OVERCOMING *Rejection*

ONE SCRIPTURE AT A TIME

30-DAY JOURNAL

This scripture writing journal belongs to:

_____

Watersprings
PUBLISHING

Overcoming Rejection, One Scripture at a Time

Published by Watersprings Media House, LLC.

P.O. Box 1284

Olive Branch, MS 38654

www.waterspringsmedia.com

© 2018 Copyrights Watersprings Media House. All rights reserved.

No portion of this book may be reproduced, stored in a retrieval system or transmitted in any form or by any means (electronic, mechanical, photocopy, recording, scanning, or other), except for brief quotations in critical reviews of articles, without the prior written permission of the writer.

Scripture quotations credited to NIV are from the Holy Bible, New International Version. Copyright © 1973, 1978, 1984, 2011 by Biblica, Inc. Used by permission. All rights reserved worldwide.

ISBN 13: 978-1-948877-15-2

Introduction

There are some issues of the heart that often go undealt with for many years. Rejection is one of them. Rejection is like a poison to the soul. It maliciously eats away at a person's self-esteem, self-worth and self-identity. We can experience the rejection from others (divorce, job, friend, family), or even impose self-rejection from shame or guilt. The truth is, all of us at one point in our lives have been the object of rejection. It often stings when it occurs, but we get over it. At times, there is some rejection that digs into the core of your heart that can leave feelings of worthlessness, anger, bitterness or defensiveness. People who are rejected tend to reject others as a defense mechanism. Even Jesus was rejected by His disciples and religious leaders. However, it is through the redeeming love of God that we are made whole.

How to Use this Scripture Writing Journal

As you use this journal, for the next 30 days, you will discover God's love and your identity in Christ. I encourage you to allow the Spirit of the living God to breathe into you every day. This journal provides four sections each day to write from the provided scripture:

Write - As you write the Word of God, allow it to penetrate your heart and mind afresh, even if it is a familiar scripture.

Listen - Listen to your heart, good, bad or indifferent and simply write. Then listen to the heart of God through that scripture and/or in that moment and write what you hear or what you understand from that scripture.

Pray - Next, take a moment to reconcile your heart and thoughts with God's words, then write a prayer from your heart. Acknowledge who God is and where you are, thanking and asking God for what you need in that moment.

My Affirmation - I've discovered that speaking positively, declaring and decreeing words of faith and affirmation will encourage you and shift your thinking. At the end of each entry write a personal affirmation. Take it a step further, put it on a post-it note, your cell phone screen or make it your daily hashtag on social media. Speak it and repeat it until you feel a difference in your spirit.

Athena C. Shack

#IAMHIS

You, dear children, are from God and have overcome them, because the one who is in you is greater than the one who is in the world.

1 John 4:4

Write the Word

Listen to the Word

Pray the Word

My Affirmation:

*Though my father and mother forsake me,
the Lord will receive me.*

Psalm 27:10

Write the Word

Listen to the Word

Pray the Word

My Affirmation:

"No weapon forged against you will prevail, and you will refute every tongue that accuses you. This is the heritage of the servants of the Lord, and this is their vindication from me," declares the Lord.

Isaiah 54:17

Write the Word

Listen to the Word

Pray the Word

My Affirmation:

Whoever believes in him is not condemned, but whoever does not believe stands condemned already because they have not believed in the name of God's one and only Son.

John 3:18

Write the Word

Listen to the Word

Pray the Word

My Affirmation:

For the eyes of the Lord range throughout the earth to strengthen those whose hearts are fully committed to him.

2 Chronicles 16:9a

Write the Word

Listen to the Word

Pray the Word

My Affirmation:

*In you, Lord, I have taken refuge;
let me never be put to shame;
deliver me in your righteousness.*

Psalm 31:1

Write the Word

Listen to the Word

Pray the Word

My Affirmation:

*Hatred stirs up conflict,
but love covers over all wrongs.*
Proverbs 10:12

Write the Word

Listen to the Word

Pray the Word

My Affirmation:

For he chose us in him before the creation of the world to be holy and blameless in his sight. In love he predestined us for adoption to sonship through Jesus Christ, in accordance with his pleasure and will— to the praise of his glorious grace, which he has freely given us in the One he loves.

Ephesians 1:4-6

Write the Word

Listen to the Word

Pray the Word

My Affirmation:

*The Lord your God is with you,
the Mighty Warrior who saves.
He will take great delight in you;
in his love he will no longer rebuke you,
but will rejoice over you with singing.*

Zephaniah 3:17

Write the Word

Listen to the Word

Pray the Word

My Affirmation:

*But love your enemies, do good to them,
and lend to them without expecting
to get anything back. Then your
reward will be great, and you will
be children of the Most High, because
he is kind to the ungrateful and wicked.*

Luke 6:35

Write the Word

Listen to the Word

Pray the Word

My Affirmation:

Let them give thanks to the Lord for his unfailing love and his wonderful deeds for mankind, for he satisfies the thirsty and fills the hungry with good things.

Psalm 107:8–9

Write the Word

Listen to the Word

Pray the Word

My Affirmation:

*Your love, Lord, reaches to the heavens,
your faithfulness to the skies.
Your righteousness is like the highest
mountains, your justice like the great deep.
You, Lord, preserve both people
and animals.*

Psalm 36:5–6

Write the Word

Listen to the Word

Pray the Word

My Affirmation:

Anyone who claims to be in the light but hates a brother or sister is still in the darkness. Anyone who loves their brother and sister lives in the light, and there is nothing in them to make them stumble.

1 John 2:9–10

Write the Word

Listen to the Word

Pray the Word

My Affirmation:

*See what great love the Father
has lavished on us, that we should
be called children of God!
And that is what we are!
The reason the world does not
know us is that it did not know him.*

1 John 3:1

Write the Word

Listen to the Word

Pray the Word

My Affirmation:

*You have not given me into
the hands of the enemy but have
set my feet in a spacious place.*

Psalm 31:8

Write the Word

Listen to the Word

Pray the Word

My Affirmation:

No, in all these things we are more than conquerors through him who loved us. For I am convinced that neither death nor life, neither angels nor demons, neither the present nor the future, nor any powers, neither height nor depth, nor anything else in all creation, will be able to separate us from the love of God that is in Christ Jesus our Lord.

Romans 8:37–39

Write the Word

Listen to the Word

Pray the Word

My Affirmation:

*As you come to him, the living Stone—
rejected by humans but chosen by God
and precious to him...*
　　1 Peter 2:4

Write the Word

Listen to the Word

Pray the Word

My Affirmation:

The thief comes only to steal and kill and destroy; I have come that they may have life, and have it to the full.

John 10:10

Write the Word

Listen to the Word

Pray the Word

My Affirmation:

*I press on toward the goal to win
the prize for which God has called me
heavenward in Christ Jesus.*

Philippians 3:14

Write the Word

Listen to the Word

Pray the Word

My Affirmation:

*Can a mother forget the baby
at her breast and have no compassion
on the child she has borne? Though
she may forget, I will not forget you!*

Isaiah 49:15

Write the Word

Listen to the Word

Pray the Word

My Affirmation:

We know that anyone born of God does not continue to sin; the One who was born of God keeps them safe, and the evil one cannot harm them.

1 John 5:18

Write the Word

Listen to the Word

Pray the Word

My Affirmation:

*So if the Son sets you free,
you will be free indeed.*

John 8:36

Write the Word

Listen to the Word

Pray the Word

My Affirmation:

For the Lord will not reject his people; he will never forsake his inheritance.

Psalm 94:14

Write the Word

Listen to the Word

Pray the Word

My Affirmation:

And the God of all grace, who called you to his eternal glory in Christ, after you have suffered a little while, will himself restore you and make you strong, firm and steadfast.

1 Peter 5:10

Write the Word

Listen to the Word

Pray the Word

My Affirmation:

*The stone the builders rejected
has become the cornerstone.*

Psalm 118:22

Write the Word

Listen to the Word

Pray the Word

My Affirmation:

What, then, shall we say in response to these things? If God is for us, who can be against us?

Romans 8:31

Write the Word

Listen to the Word

Pray the Word

My Affirmation:

*For you created my inmost being;
you knit me together in my mother's
womb. I praise you because I am fearfully
and wonderfully made; your works
are wonderful, I know that full well.*

Psalm 139:13–14

Write the Word

Listen to the Word

Pray the Word

My Affirmation:

*Therefore, there is now no condemnation
for those who are in Christ Jesus,
because through Christ Jesus the law
of the Spirit who gives life has set
you free from the law of sin and death.*

Romans 8:1–2

Write the Word

Listen to the Word

Pray the Word

My Affirmation:

...being confident of this, that he who began a good work in you will carry it on to completion until the day of Christ Jesus.

Philippians 1:6

Write the Word

Listen to the Word

Pray the Word

My Affirmation:

In him we were also chosen, having been predestined according to the plan of him who works out everything in conformity with the purpose of his will, in order that we, who were the first to put our hope in Christ, might be for the praise of his glory.

Ephesians 1:11–12

Write the Word

Listen to the Word

Pray the Word

My Affirmation:

MORE JOURNALS

www.WriteListenPray.com